Classic Collection

20,000 Leagues Under the Sea

JULES VERNE

Adapted by Ronne Randall · Illustrated by Andy Catling

QEB Publishing

A Mysterious Sea Monster

I am French scientist Pierre Aronnax, assistant professor of marine biology at the Paris Museum of Natural History. In 1866, sailors from many countries began saying they had seen a strange, huge sea monster lurking below the waves. It was bigger than the biggest whale—some said it was as much as a mile long!—and it was faster, too. At times, it even seemed to be glowing! More than once it crashed into ships, causing serious damage. Was it a terrible sea creature or a gigantic man-made war machine? No one knew!

I first heard about the mysterious marine menace when, in April 1867, the colossal object rammed a British ocean liner, ripping open its hull and putting many lives at risk. People all over the world now wanted the monster found and destroyed.

I was in New York when the U.S. government decided to send out an expedition to find the monster and thanks to my specialist knowledge, they invited me to join them. Now perhaps I could confirm my belief that the creature was a gigantic narwhal whose long, hard tusk might easily pierce a ship's hull.

So, in July 1867, I boarded the frigate the *Abraham Lincoln,* along with my brave and loyal servant, Conseil. The ship's commander, Captain Farragut, was there to greet us. "You are most welcome, Professor," he said. "Your cabin is ready for you."

Captain Farragut and his loyal crew were all eager to hunt down the monster, harpoon it, and haul it onboard.

The ship's most skilled harpooner was Ned Land, a tall, brave Canadian. He was deadly accurate with his harpoon, and we were lucky to have him onboard.

We made our way down to South America, around Cape Horn, and north into the Pacific. Weeks passed with no sign of the monster.

After three long months at sea, even the most enthusiastic crew members were discouraged. Finally, Captain Farragut announced that if nothing happened within the next three days, we would head for home.

On the evening of the third day, Conseil and I were talking on deck when Ned Land called out, "Look out there! It's approaching!"

There, a short distance from the ship, we saw an eerie glow beneath the water's surface. The monster, at last! It stayed close to us all night. At dawn it surfaced, and the *Abraham Lincoln* gave chase.

We raced furiously after it, with Ned Land holding his harpoon at the ready. What a chase it was! We even tried shooting it with guns, but the bullets just bounced off.

"That animal must be clad in six-inch iron plates!" the captain exclaimed.

It led us on all day and long into the night. At last it stopped and lay still, seemingly exhausted.

The Floating Island

Captain Farragut gave orders for the ship to move ahead slowly and quietly. When we were about 20 feet from the creature, Ned Land suddenly released his harpoon. It struck with a loud clanging sound, as if it were hitting hard metal.

All at once two enormous torrents of water gushed onto the deck, knocking men down—and throwing me overboard. I swam toward the boat, crying desperately for help. But my mouth filled with water, and I began to sink.

Suddenly, I felt someone grab me—it was Conseil, my faithful servant.

"Lean on me," he said. "I will help you swim." He told me the *Abraham Lincoln* had a broken rudder. I begged Conseil to leave me and save himself, but he refused. Instead, he called out for help. Miraculously, someone answered.

It was Ned Land. He had survived by clinging to some sort of floating island. As we struggled toward him, we could see that the "island" was actually the monster—and that it was made of metal plates! This was no living monster, but a man-made vessel, some kind of submarine craft. Shivering, we clung there all night. Just after daybreak, one of the iron plates rose up and a man appeared. Obviously shocked to see us, he disappeared quickly. Seconds later, eight men came and dragged us all inside.

Held Captive

We were locked in a room so dark that we could not even see our own hands. The floating island had become our floating prison.

After half an hour, the door opened, the room was flooded with light, and two men appeared. They spoke a language none of us could understand. Nor could they understand any of the languages we spoke to them— French, English, German, and even Latin—so they left.

Moments later, the door opened again and a servant entered. He brought us clothes like those worn by the men we had seen—tunics and pants of a strange material. Then he returned with food for us, all in covered dishes. The food was fish of many different kinds, some of which I did not recognize.

After dinner, we all fell asleep. I was the first to wake up, but I didn't know how long we'd been sleeping. I wondered how much longer we could go on breathing in this enclosed underwater space. Then I felt a sea breeze! I realized at once that the boat had surfaced like a whale to take in fresh air.

By now, the others were awake. Ned, still hungry and frustrated at being confined, began talking frantically about escaping. When a steward entered our room, Ned lunged at him and held him pinned to the floor.

I was about to rescue the poor man when, to my amazement, a voice said, in perfect French, "Calm yourself, Mr. Land. And you, Professor, please listen to me."

Captain Nemo

It was the commander of the vessel. He introduced himself as Captain Nemo.

"Annoying circumstances have brought you into my presence," he said, sounding irritated. "The *Abraham Lincoln* has been pursuing me, and I therefore have the right to treat you all as enemies. I could sink beneath the water and forget that you ever existed if I so wish. Do you not agree?"

"I'm sure there is no need for that," I cried. "Let's discuss this as civilized men."

"But I am not a civilized man! For my own reasons, I have left human society," Captain Nemo declared. "I no longer obey its laws. On the *Nautilus*, the only law is mine."

Nemo did, however, agree to give us our freedom onboard his ship, as long as we stayed locked in our cabins when ordered and we promised not to escape.

Ned Land was furious and refused to promise to do such a thing. I, however, felt differently. Nemo had found my weak spot—this was a rare opportunity to study underwater life in great detail and discover many wonderful things. How could I resist?

Captain Nemo invited me to have breakfast with him. The dining table was spread with an amazing array of seafood.

"The sea supplies all my needs," Nemo said, noticing my amazement.

A Tour of the Nautilus

After breakfast, Captain Nemo gave me a tour of the vessel, starting with his library. Tall bookcases held thousands of volumes on every imaginable subject.

Next we entered a vast living room with paintings by the world's great masters on the walls. There was an organ, too, scattered with sheet music. In the center of the room was a beautiful fountain in the shape of a giant shell. Surrounding it were glass cases filled with rare marine specimens: soft sponges from Syria, many superb corals and starfish, delicate and fragile shells, such as the white bivalve, and pearls of the greatest beauty and color, to name just a few.

"I collected them all myself," Nemo told me. "There is not a sea in the world that I have not visited."

The captain then took me to his own cabin, which contained the instruments used to navigate the *Nautilus* and control its unique power system.

Nemo also showed me where, when the ship surfaced, a man could climb out onto a platform and breathe fresh air.

We moved on, passing through the ship's kitchen, which had equipment for turning seawater into drinking water. There was also a bathroom with hot and cold running water.

Nemo patiently answered all of my questions about the *Nautilus*, but he kept silent about personal matters. He had created his own world here, with everything he could possibly need or want. I wondered why.

Captain Nemo invited me to see exactly how the *Nautilus* worked.

"My secrets are safe," he said. "After all, you are never going to leave this boat."

In his cabin, he spread out diagrams showing the structure of the *Nautilus* and its inner workings. He had had all of the parts built in different countries and assembled on a remote desert island.

"You must be very wealthy," I commented.

"Yes," he said quietly. "I have more money than you could possibly imagine." There was no pride and no pleasure in his voice. Clearly, his riches had not made him happy.

Nemo asked me to go with him to the platform, where we stood looking out over the north Pacific. The sea was calm, the sky clear, and there was a slight breeze in the air. There was nothing in sight.

"Today, at noon, our underwater voyage of exploration will begin," Nemo told me.

I then joined Ned and Conseil, who were viewing the colorful underwater world through a huge window—it was a truly wonderful sight!

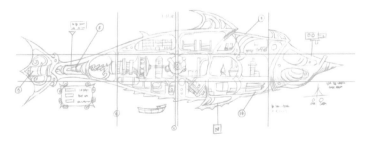

An Underwater Hunting Trip

I desperately wanted to learn more about Nemo: where was he from? Why was he so bitter about human society? But he had said all he was going to say to me. For the next week or so, no one even saw him.

Then, on returning to my cabin one day, I found a letter on the table. It was from Captain Nemo, inviting me, Conseil, and Ned to hunt in the forests of Crespo Island.

Ned was excited at the prospect of hunting and also at the possibility of escape once we were on land. When he learned that the forests were under water, he refused to go. Conseil and I, however, were eager for the experience.

We were given globelike helmets to wear, along with waterproof clothing and thick rubber boots. Breathing tanks were strapped to our backs, and we were given lamps and guns that could shoot under water.

I could not imagine how we would be able to move with all of this heavy clothing and equipment, but as soon as we stepped out into the water, moving became almost effortless. The water took all of the weight, and we walked easily along the ocean floor.

The fine sand on the seabed beneath our feet reflected the sunlight from above, even at a depth of thirty feet. As we walked toward the forest, a rainbow of colors appeared before us—there were plants, rocks, corals, and sea animals of many different kinds. It was a feast for the eyes, and Conseil and I were dazzled.

We walked for about an hour and a half, going deeper all of the time. Suddenly, Nemo stopped and pointed.

"Behold, the forest of Crespo Island," he said.

The forest was made of tall, arching treelike plants, and the ground was carpeted with herbs. There was so much to explore and study!

After several hours of examining the plants, I sat down to rest and soon fell asleep. When I awoke, I was terrified to see a huge sea spider, several feet tall, ready to spring at me. I was very relieved when Nemo appeared and began to battle the beast with his rifle. For all of its beauty, the undersea world held many dangers.

Several more hours passed, and it was time to go back to our ship. Along the way, Nemo shot two magnificent creatures: a sea otter, whose glossy coat must have been very valuable, and a large bird called an albatross that was flying just above the water. We saw some dogfish, which could have crushed us in their terrible jaws. Luckily, their eyesight was so poor that they swam past us.

We made it safely back to the *Nautilus*. Exhausted, all I wanted was food and sleep. I knew that I would dream of all of the marvels I had seen that day.

Stuck on a Reef

Many weeks passed. We made our way through rocky passages between uninhabited islands and passed several shipwrecks. One morning I discovered that we were now approaching the Torres Straits, which led to the Indian Ocean.

We knew that getting through these straits could be dangerous, and sure enough, the *Nautilus* hit a coral reef and became stuck. It would be a few days before the tides rose high enough to float us out, so Nemo suggested that Ned, Conseil, and I might want to row to the nearby island of Papua New Guinea and explore it.

Ned was excited. "This could be our chance to escape!" he exclaimed.

Personally, I had no desire to escape into the wilds of a place I knew almost nothing about. But all of us were very eager to be on land again.

Ned was especially eager to hunt. "I am desperate to taste some meat, or anything that doesn't come from the sea!" he said.

So the next morning, the dinghy was unlocked, and we rowed the two miles to the island.

How delighted we were to set foot on land again! We found some fruit-bearing trees, and we collected as many coconuts, pineapples, bananas, and mangoes as we could. After enjoying some of the fruit ourselves, we took the rest back to the *Nautilus* that evening.

Our Island Adventure

The three of us headed out again the next day, this time to hunt. We shot birds, wild hogs, and tree kangaroo and had a splendid dinner of roasted meat and sweet, juicy fruit. What a feast!

As we were enjoying our meal, a stone fell suddenly at our feet. Scarcely a moment later, another flew toward us, knocking a roasted pigeon out of Conseil's hand.

We were being attacked!

We ran for the dinghy amid a shower of arrows. As we rowed back to the *Nautilus*, we realized that the Papuans were chasing us in canoes.
We barely managed to escape with our lives.

When I told Nemo that we had been attacked by the natives, he said that I was wrong to be scared.

"Even if all of the natives of Papua were to gather on this shore, the *Nautilus* would have nothing to fear from their attacks," he said.

I still felt uncertain, but the next day, I understood why Nemo was so confident. The Papuans returned and one reached out to touch the stair rail of the *Nautilus*. At once, he was thrown backward by some invisible force. It was not a rail, but a cable charged with electricity! It was clear no one could board the ship, and so the Papuans fled. The tide soon rose enough for the *Nautilus* to float off the coral reef. Our island adventure was over.

An Underwater Graveyard

Our voyage continued through the Indian Ocean. One day Captain Nemo told Ned, Conseil, and me that we must stay locked in our cabins for the day. He would not tell us why.

The next morning, Nemo asked if I had medical training. When I said yes, he took me to a cabin in the crew's quarters, where a man lay badly injured. His head was wrapped in bandages, which I unwound carefully.

His wound was very serious—he must have been hit with a heavy blunt object that had crushed his skull. His eyes bulged, and his pulse was weak.

"I'm afraid there is nothing I can do," I told Nemo. "He will not last more than a few hours."

To my surprise, Captain Nemo's eyes filled with tears, and he turned away. I was haunted by thoughts of the dying man for the rest of the day.

The next morning, Nemo asked us to put on diving suits and accompany him and some crew members outside. We walked out into a spectacular kingdom of coral, with a carpet of flowers under our feet.

We came to a vast open space surrounded by towering underwater trees, and here a crew member began to dig a hole. This place was obviously a cemetery. We had come to bury the man I had seen the day before.

"Your dead sleep peacefully," I remarked to Captain Nemo. "At least they are out of the reach of sharks."

"Yes," replied Nemo, "of sharks and men."

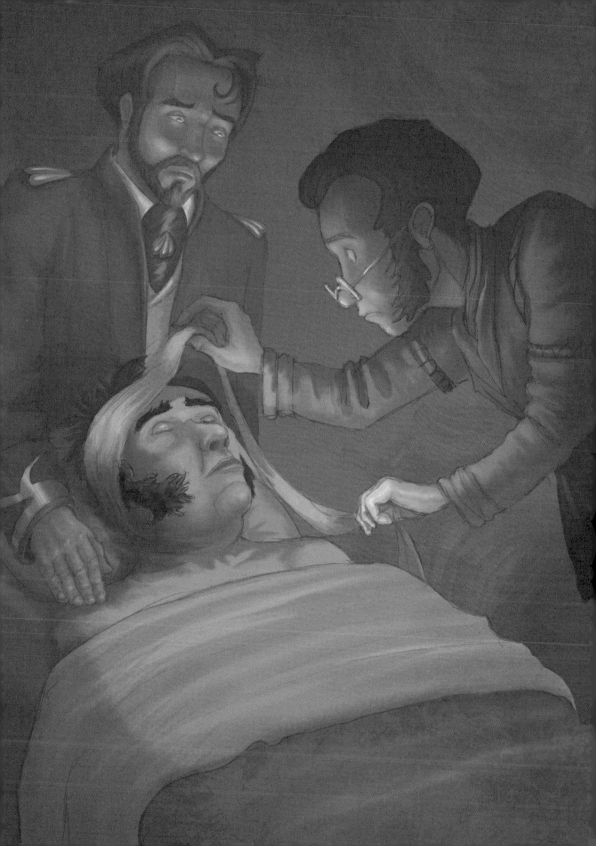

A Wonder of Nature

By late January, we were nearing the island of Ceylon, which is known for its pearl fisheries. We were delighted when Captain Nemo offered us a chance to see them. We knew that there were sharks in these waters, but we were not about to let that stop us.

Just after dawn the next morning, we put on our diving suits and set off with Nemo. Soon we were at the breeding grounds of the oysters that produced the pearls. There seemed to be countless numbers of them clinging to the rocks, some of them as much as five inches across. I knew that the larger ones were older and had bigger pearls inside them.

Captain Nemo seemed to know where he was going, and we followed him down a steep incline. Suddenly, a huge grotto opened out before us, and in the center was an oyster of gigantic proportions. Inside the creature's half-open shell I glimpsed a gleaming pearl as big as a coconut! I reached out to touch it, but Nemo stopped me.

"I have been coming here for many years," he told me. "No one else knows about this creature. Each year the pearl grows bigger, and when the time is right, I will take it for my collection."

After admiring this wonder of nature for some time, Captain Nemo was ready to leave, and we followed him out of the grotto.

Shark Attack!

On our way back to the *Nautilus*, we spotted a pearl diver and stopped to watch him. He was clearly very poor. His only equipment was a bag for collecting oysters and a stone tied to his foot to help his descent. He risked his life with each dive. We watched in fascination, until suddenly the man began to swim frantically to the surface. An enormous shark was chasing the terrified diver!

The man tried to dodge the monster but couldn't escape its swishing tail, which knocked him unconscious. I was frozen with terror, but Nemo bolted bravely forward and sank his dagger into the shark! As the water turned red with blood, the captain struggled mightily with the monster until Ned rushed forward and plunged his harpoon into the beast's belly.

Released from the grip of the shark, Nemo rushed to the pearl diver. He cut the cord holding the stone and pulled the diver to the surface. We all followed and remained by his boat until he came to.

We were astonished to see Captain Nemo draw a bag of pearls out of his diving suit and place it in the diver's hand—a gift from one man of the sea to another.

Later, thinking about the day's events, I realized that Captain Nemo was braver than I had imagined. Despite his harsh words about human society, there was definitely kindness in his heart.

The Greek Island

Over the next weeks, we moved through the Indian Ocean and the Red Sea. By mid February, we were in the Mediterranean approaching the island of Crete.

When I left America, the Cretan people had recently rebelled against their Turkish oppressors. I wondered how they were coping but assumed the situation wouldn't be of interest to Captain Nemo. However, once more, I was about to glimpse a rare example of his concern for the poor and needy.

One day, I was studying some fish through the glass panels in the living room. Suddenly, a man swam into view! Thinking he must be a shipwrecked sailor who needed help, I called Captain Nemo.

"Do not be concerned," he assured me. "That is Nicholas Pesca, a local diver. Everyone in these islands knows him."

To my surprise, the two men exchanged hand signals, and the diver returned to the surface.

Nemo then opened a chest that I could see held many valuable gold bars. He removed some bars, put them in a safe, and then wrote a Greek address on the lid.

That night, when the *Nautilus* rose to the surface, I heard someone unlock the dinghy and row away. Two hours later, the boat returned, and the *Nautilus* dipped below the waves once more.

"So," I thought to myself, "the safe has been delivered—but to whom?"

Ned's Plan

Our journey around the Mediterranean continued, and I eagerly studied the plentiful species of fish outside the *Nautilus*. We witnessed many natural wonders and experienced the underwater eruption of a volcano. This caused the *Nautilus* to become uncomfortably warm!

Sometimes we found shipwrecks, particularly as we approached the narrow Strait of Gibraltar. Luckily, we made our way through safely, and at last we were in the open waters of the Atlantic.

One afternoon, Ned told me he planned to escape before Nemo took us to some other strange place.

"Tonight we will be only a few miles off the Spanish coast," he said. "It's the perfect time to make our escape. This evening, when Nemo is in his cabin, we must launch the dinghy and row to Spain."

"I am with you, Ned," I said. Though I doubted Nemo could hold us forever, he was far too unpredictable, and we might not get a chance like this again.

"Good," he said, shaking my hand. "After dinner, go to the living room and wait for my signal."

I prayed silently that he knew what he was doing.

Sunken Treasure

That night, as I waited nervously for Ned's signal, I felt the *Nautilus* come to a sudden stop. The door of the living room opened, and Nemo entered.

"Ah, Professor, I was looking for you," he said. I knew immediately that our escape plans were ruined.

Nemo began telling me a story about some Spanish ships that were sailing back to Cádiz from the Americas in 1702, loaded with treasure from the New World. When an English fleet attacked, the admiral in charge of escorting the Spanish convoy burned all of the ships rather than let the treasure fall into enemy hands.

"We are now at the spot where the treasure lies," Nemo told me, glancing toward the glass panel. Outside, I could see crew members in diving suits emptying cases filled with gold, silver, and precious jewels.

"This is how I became so wealthy," said Nemo. "I pick up what men have lost—not just here, but at shipwrecks all over the world. Did you know the sea contained such riches, Professor?"

"Doesn't this treasure belong to the Spanish people?" I asked. "Why should you get rich at their expense?"

"These riches are not just for me," Nemo said. "I put this wealth to good use. It finds its way to the poor and suffering of the world."

Suddenly, I remembered the safe filled with gold bars that had left the ship in the Greek islands. Now I understood where it had gone.

The Lost Continent

The next evening, Captain Nemo invited me to walk with him along the seabed so that I could see what it looked like in darkness. We left late at night. The only light was a tiny red glow in the distance. It grew brighter as we got closer, and I could see that it came from behind a huge underwater mountain.

As we began to climb the mountain, a boulder-strewn path led us between tangled branches of dead trees. My blood froze when I saw giant crabs and lobsters lurching toward us. But Nemo was speeding up the steep path, and I had to race to keep up with him.

As we climbed higher, and the light grew brighter, I realized that the mountain was actually a volcano. Like a giant torch, its red-hot lava streams gave everything nearby an eerie red glow.

Looking beyond its crater, I gasped in astonishment. There below us lay the remains of an ancient town, its once-fine buildings in ruins. Where was this? I turned to Nemo and watched as he traced a single word on a rock: ATLANTIS.

This, then, was the legendary lost continent that had once joined Africa to America. Destroyed by an earthquake, it had been lost beneath the sea. I tried to fix every detail in my brain, for I knew that I would never again have the chance to see this wonder. Surely I was one of the luckiest men alive.

The South Pole

I did not forget Atlantis. But over the next few days, Conseil and I became absorbed in studying the amazing variety of fish that swam alongside our ship. As well as sharks and rays, which we had seen before, there were brightly colored species that seemed to light up when the sun hit them.

Weeks passed, and we continued to make our way south through the Atlantic. By mid March, we were nearing Antarctica, and as we went farther south, we began to see icebergs that gleamed with colored stripes. Some were pale green, others a delicate purple. They looked like enormous jewels when the sun shone through them.

When we were close enough, we rowed ashore to look at the Antarctic wildlife. I was especially interested in the seals and walrus, as well as the penguins that crowded the ice. Though they are graceful swimmers, the penguins are slow and clumsy out of the water.

Captain Nemo was determined to take us all the way to the South Pole, and toward the end of the month, he succeeded. We climbed to the top of a peak from which we could see a vast expanse of ice all around us. At noon, Nemo took a reading on his instruments.

"The South Pole," he said in a solemn voice. He then unfurled a flag—a gold "N" on a background of black —and announced, "I claim this part of the globe as the new domain of Captain Nemo."

Icebound

Once he had achieved his ambition, Captain Nemo was ready to leave Antarctica. I wondered what surprises we now had in store.

I didn't have to wonder for long. That night, a violent shock woke me. What could have happened? Before long, Captain Nemo told us the bad news.

"There has been a serious accident," he said. "An iceberg has collapsed around the *Nautilus*, trapping us. We must free the ship within forty-eight hours or we will all suffocate from lack of oxygen."

Ned immediately volunteered to hack away at the ice. "I'm as good with a pickax as a harpoon," he said. Everyone joined him, working in teams around the clock. We made little progress, however.

It was exhausting work and the cold made it impossible to stay out for long. But at least the air in the underwater outfit was fresh. Inside the *Nautilus*, the air was stale and poisonous, choking us. Time was running out!

Eventually, Nemo saved us. He came up with the idea of using boiling water to melt the ice surrounding the ship. Then he filled up its storage areas with water, making it heavier, so it sank and cracked the ice below.

Just in time, the *Nautilus* broke free of its icy prison. The hatch was opened, and we filled our lungs with sea air once more.

The Giant Squid

We were all grateful to be alive, and by the time we had sailed north past Cape Horn, we had put our terrible Antarctic adventure out of our minds.

Once again, Ned began talking about escaping. But for the next few weeks we were too far from land even to think of leaving the ship.

Toward the end of April, approaching the Bahamas, we saw a thick bed of seaweed. I knew this meant that dangerous squids were lurking nearby. Sure enough, I soon counted seven of the creatures outside one of the *Nautilus*'s windows.

Moments later, the engine stopped and our ship stopped moving forward. Somehow a giant squid must have trapped us in its monstrous tentacles.

Captain Nemo gathered ten crew members to help him get rid of the monsters. Ned joined them with his harpoon, and Conseil and I grabbed hatchets.

As soon as the *Nautilus*'s hatch was opened, two strong tentacles reached down and grabbed one of the crew in a stranglehold. Captain Nemo bolted out, and we followed him. As we battled against the giant squid, it sent out jets of black ink, that burned and blinded us.

When we could see again, the monster squid had disappeared, along with the unlucky crew member.

Nemo wept for his lost crew member, both that day and in the days to come. Once again, I saw that he was not as cold and hard hearted as he seemed.

Captain Nemo grieved for the next few weeks, and rarely left his cabin.

Ned now talked constantly of leaving the *Nautilus,* and I finally agreed to speak to Nemo. Maybe, in his grief, he would change his mind and let us go.

But nothing had changed. "I have already told you," he said angrily, "once you board the *Nautilus,* you never leave!"

The *Nautilus* was nearing the New England coast, and, undaunted by Nemo, we planned to head for the shore when we were close enough.

But luck was not with us. A hurricane blew up, throwing the ship off course. Our hopes of escaping were shattered.

A short time later, disaster struck again. As we moved east across the Atlantic, a warship began firing at us. It had no flag, so we could not tell where it was from.

Nemo did not hesitate. Raising his black flag, he bellowed, "Ship of a cursed nation, I will destroy you!"

Nemo took the *Nautilus* below the surface and repeatedly rammed the warship's hull. Finally, in a huge explosion, the ship sank, taking her entire crew with her.

I was horrified at this loss of life and Nemo's heartlessness. The *Nautilus* was safe, but were we safe from Nemo? His rage and madness were terrifying.

The Final Escape

An air of doom now hung over the *Nautilus*. Then, early one morning, Ned came to my cabin.

"We're leaving—tonight," he whispered. "We're twenty miles from land. We have to risk it."

I agreed. Our stay on the *Nautilus* had become unbearable.

That night, while Nemo was playing the organ in the living room, we scrambled onto the platform.

A storm had blown up, and now we were close to a churning whirlpool. The dinghy rocked dangerously as we climbed in. We knew it was foolish to launch ourselves into such a raging sea, but we had no choice.

Suddenly, there was a loud crash, and the dinghy was wrenched away from the *Nautilus*. Something struck me on the head, and everything went black.

I awoke in a fisherman's hut in Norway. Ned and Conseil were beside me, both safe and well.

I have no idea how we got here or what has become of the *Nautilus* and Captain Nemo. I hope they survived the whirlpool and continue to explore the oceans in peace. They have given me a marvelous gift. In ten months, I have gone 20,000 leagues, traveling the world under the sea, and I have seen unimaginable marvels.

Perhaps no one will believe my story. But it is true. There is a passage in the Bible that says, "That which is far off and very deep, who can find it out?" Only two men—Captain Nemo and I.

About the author

Jules Gabriel Verne was born in France in 1828.
Jules attended a boarding school as a child, where he
showed great interest in travel and exploration. Much to the
disappointment of his wealthy family, he became distracted
by his story writing and began to fail at other subjects. He
moved to Paris to study in 1863, and there he met many other
influential writers and his future publisher. Along with *20,000
Leagues*, he is best known for the novels *A Journey to the Center
of the Earth* and *Around the World in Eighty Days*. Famous
for pioneering the genre of science fiction, he wrote about
travel under the water and travel by air before they were even
invented. Jules died in March 1905 at the age of 77.

Other titles in the *Classic Collection* series:

Alice's Adventures in Wonderland • *Little Women*
The Three Musketeers • *Treasure Island*
Heidi • *Pinocchio* • *The Wizard of Oz*

Editors: Su Box and Victoria Garrard • Designer: Andrea Mills

Copyright © QEB Publishing 2012

First published in the United States in 2012 by
QEB Publishing, Inc.
3 Wrigley, Suite A
Irvine, CA 92618

www.qed-publishing.co.uk

A CIP record for this book is available from the Library of Congress.

ISBN 978 1 60992 302 0

Printed in China